round

KIRSTEN FISHER

FABRIC ART BOWLS

Sew Artisan Bowls with Infinite Possibilities

C&T PUBLISHING
Another Maker Inspired!

Text copyright © 2023 by Kirsten Fisher

Photography and artwork copyright © 2023 by C&T Publishing, Inc.

Publisher: Amy Barrett-Daffin

Creative Director: Gailen Runge

Senior Editor: Roxane Cerda

Editor: Madison Moore

Technical Editor: Debbie Rodgers

Cover/Book Designer: April Mostek

Production Coordinator: Tim Manibusan

Illustrator: Linda Johnson

Photography Coordinator: Lauren Herberg

Photography Assistant: Rachel Ackley

Photography by Lauren Herberg, Gailen Runge of C&T Publishing, Inc., unless otherwise noted

Published by C&T Publishing, Inc., P.O. Box 1456, Lafayette, CA 94549

Library of Congress Cataloging-in-Publication Data

Names: Fisher, Kirsten, 1950- author.

Title: Round fabric art bowls : sew artisan bowls with infinite possibilities / Kirsten Fisher.

Description: Lafayette, CA : C&T Publishing, Another Maker Inspired, [2023] | Summary: "Learn how to construct fabric bowls and how to adjust the size so you can create your own inspiring piece in the size you want. Inside are six 16" bowl projects that include machine sewing and piecing, modified paper piecing, applique, English Paper Piecing, and more for eye-catching results"-- Provided by publisher.

Identifiers: LCCN 2022062071 | ISBN 9781644032480 (trade paperback) | ISBN 9781644032497 (ebook)

Subjects: LCSH: Fabric bowls. | Machine sewing. | Bowls (Tableware)

Classification: LCC TT835 .F5725 2023 | DDC 646.2/044--dc23/eng/20230203

LC record available at https://lccn.loc.gov/2022062071

Printed in the USA

10 9 8 7 6 5 4 3 2 1

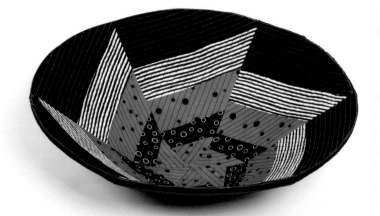

DEDICATION

Over the past 28 years, the Brooklyn Quilters Guild has been a constant source of support and inspiration for me. I happened upon their first guild show and realized not only that I had found my medium but that there was a group of people with a shared interest that I could be part of.

The guild started in 1993 with just 30 members, has now grown to about 200 members and is as diverse as Brooklyn itself.

The volunteers of guilds around the country organize meetings and quilt shows, write the newsletters, and make the many charity quilts. Most of all, they help keep the art of quilting alive so that it can be enjoyed by everyone.

This book is dedicated to the Brooklyn Guild and the many volunteers who over the years have made the guild what it is today.

ACKNOWLEDGMENTS

There are many people to thank for their contributions to this book.

Thanks to Roxane Cerda, the C&T acquisitions editor who believed in my first book, *Modern Fabric Art Bowls*, and gave me the opportunity to write this second book to follow up with patterns and directions for round bowls.

Many thanks to my editor, Madison Moore, whose incredible patience and technical assistance have helped me from the very beginning of this book.

Another thank you to the many other people at C&T who worked with us on making this book.

Many thanks to my good friend Martha McDonald. Her support, calm steadiness, and clear thinking made writing this book so much easier.

And thanks to Madeleine Appell for letting me use some of her fabric.

I was lucky to come across Tres Rebecas, a craft shop in San Antonio, Texas with an incredible staff and a treasure chest of some of my favorite sold-out fabrics, some of which have been used in this book.

Since my first book, *Modern Fabric Art Bowls*, was published, many crafters from many parts of the world have become my social media friends, and I thank you for all the great pictures of your fabric bowls and the encouragement to take on this book.

My husband, Ken Fisher, isn't a crafter, but no one has encouraged me more.

contents

chapter 1

INTRODUCTION

Several years ago I took a class with Judith Doenias on how to draw your own star pattern for a quilt block. I made a block with three stars in it and sat looking at it for some time. At that time, I had just started to make square fabric bowls with interior designs based on quilt blocks.

So I decided to make the jump to a round bowl so that I could fit my star design into it. The pattern I came up with was complicated to design; because of the six seams, transforming the 2D design into a 3D one had to incorporate the points of the star, but I enjoyed the challenge.

After working on bowls with star designs, I realized that the round shape lends itself to making bowls based on flowers, and all kinds of designs began to emerge to create this book.

These bowls are easy to make, and almost all the seams can be sewn by machine. The bowls are made of two layers of double-sided fusible heavyweight interfacing: an inside layer and an outside layer. The two layers are made separately, and the bowl is completed by fusing the two layers together. All the seams are hidden within the two layers.

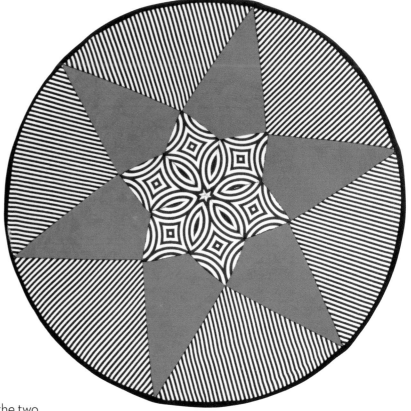

Bowl design based on star block

The pattern for the outside layer of all the bowls is the same, and it has only six seams. The pattern for the inside layer of Bowls 1 and 2 is the same as the pattern for the outside layer with minor changes. The pattern for the inside layer of Bowls 3 and 4 has an inset center circle as the base. Bowls 5 and 6 are based on a star design, and the seams of the star center are sewn by hand.

The steps to make the bowls are very simple. For the outside layer, the pattern is drawn onto heavyweight double-sided fusible interfacing using simple templates. The interfacing is cut out and fused to fabric, and the six seams are sewn. For the inside layer, the templates are traced onto heavyweight double-sided fusible interfacing. The interfacing pieces are cut out and fused to fabric. After the fabric has been trimmed to ¼″ (6mm) seam allowance, the seams are sewn together.

Chapters 2, 3, 4, and 5 are general instructions relevant to all the bowls, so it's important to start there. Chapter 6 explains how to make the outside layer, which is required for every bowl. The bowl projects are written from easiest to most difficult, and Chapter 13 is a technique chapter on how to change the size of the bowl.

There are so many ways to customize your bowl. Both the inside and outside layers can be quilted.

NOTE

Do not use water-soluble marker to draw the quilting lines.

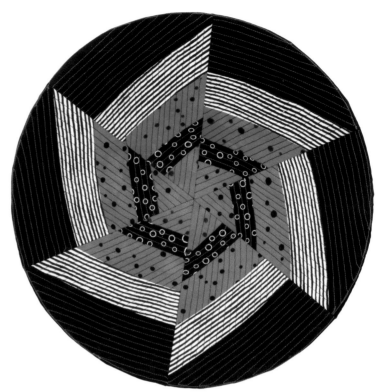

Quilted bowl

The bowl also can be painted with fabric paint.

FABRIC PAINT *It is best to paint the bowl after the inside and outside layers have been fused together. Fuse a piece of the fabric to a small piece of interfacing, and paint a sample before you paint the whole bowl.*

Painted bowl by Maj Wildschiodtz, age 7

Painted bowl by Malina Shorenstein, age 8

The bowls are primarily decorative. If you'd like to use them in other ways, a protective layer of decoupage medium like Mod Podge can be added to both the inside and outside layers after the two layers have been fused together. You can add an additional layer of water-based protective coating like polycrylic protective finish. A protective layer also can be used to secure a design that is very difficult to sew.

With all this in mind, let's get started!

Bowl with protective layer by
Maj Wildschiodtz, age 7

chapter 2

BOWL SIZES AND FABRICS

CHOOSING A BOWL

The projects are listed in this book from easiest to most difficult. Bowl 1 is a one-piece cloth bowl. Bowl 2 is a six-piece bowl. Both projects can be sewn with straight seams on a machine.

Bowl 3, the flower bowl, can be sewn on a machine with a zigzag or decorative stitch or by hand for an easy hand-sewing project.

Bowl 4 is a Dresden block bowl made from nineteen pieces that can be sewn on a machine.

In Bowl 5, the single-star bowl, and Bowl 6, the double-star bowl, the center star can be sewn by hand.

Keep these descriptions in mind when you decide which project to start with. All the patterns in this book are for bowls with a diameter of 16″ (40.6cm) and a height of 4½″ (11.4cm). If you'd like to make the bowls smaller, see Chapter 13: Changing the Size of the Bowl (page 70).

CHOOSING FABRICS

You can choose a fabric before or after you choose a bowl project. In general, bold fabrics with high contrast create exciting bowls. The process for selecting fabrics for bowls is very similar to selecting fabrics for a quilt block. The patterns in this book are for bowls made up of six identical units. In some bowls, the units meet in the center; in others, the six units surround the center. So except for Bowl 1, the center of the bowl is the focal point. Keep that in mind when choosing a fabric.

Nondirectional Fabric

Fabrics with overall designs that do not need to be oriented a certain way work well for these bowls, especially Bowl 1. To make a nondirectional fabric more interesting, consider adding appliqué designs. In this example, I added appliqué red and black circles to highlight the existing pattern on the fabric.

You should consider the best way to use the fabric you choose. In this example of a nondirectional floral pattern, decide which flower should be in the center of the bowl to make best use of the pattern. Keep in mind that some parts of the pattern will be lost to the six wedges that form the shape of the bowl.

Fabric with nondirectional design

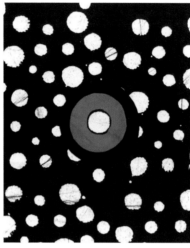

Appliqué added

Fabric used in one-piece cloth bowl

Fabric with nondirectional floral pattern

Fabric used in one-piece cloth bowl

Directional Fabric

Fabrics with directional designs work great for every bowl except Bowl 1.

The center circles of Bowl 3 and Bowl 4 are made from one piece of interfacing, so it is best to make each with one piece of fabric. You can leave the fabric as is or add appliqué or decorative stitches. If you choose to leave the fabric as is, try highlighting a single motif from the fabric's design.

Single flower motif as center circle

Decorative stitches added to center circle

The centers of Bowls 2, 5, and 6 are pieced, so they can be made interesting by fussy cutting the fabric into a secondary design. See Basic Techniques for All Bowls (page 24) to learn more about fusing directional fabrics.

Fabric with leaf motif

Stems creating simple motif

Motif creating interesting
design for final bowl

Stripes

Stripes, running in either direction, can make the center of the bowl very interesting. Even checkered patterns with both vertical and horizontal lines work great.

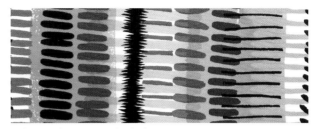

Fabric with stripes in both directions

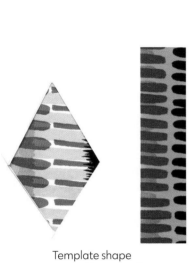

Template shape
positioned horizontally

Center star
with horizontal
lines

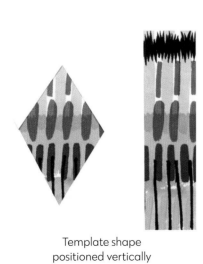

Template shape
positioned vertically

Center star
with vertical
lines

Graphic Patterns

Patterns with very strong contrast can make very interesting centers.

Fabric with graphic pattern

Curved black lines will create secondary pattern in center of bowl

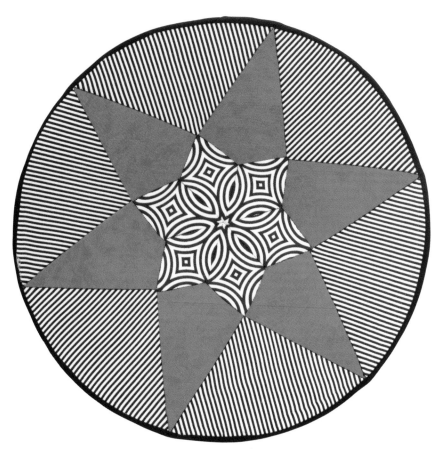

Center star with secondary pattern

chapter 3
SUPPLIES

HEAVYWEIGHT DOUBLE-SIDED FUSIBLE INTERFACING

All interfacing used for the projects in this book is heavyweight double-sided fusible interfacing. There are several brands of heavyweight double-sided fusible interfacing on the market; I have worked with both fast2fuse HEAVY Interfacing (by C&T Publishing) and 72F Peltex II Two-Sided Fusible Ultra Firm Stabilizer (by Pellon).

fast2fuse fuses to fabric with steam and a cotton heat setting on the iron. It is available by the yard at 20″ (50.8cm) wide and also in packaged pieces that are 15″ × 18″ (38.1 × 45.7cm) or 20″ × 20″ (50.8 × 50.8cm).

72F Peltex fuses to fabric with a damp cloth and an iron on wool setting. You cannot see the fabric as you fuse it to the interfacing when using this version. It is available only by the yard and is 20″ (50.8cm) wide.

It is very important that you use the same brand and weight of interfacing throughout an entire project.

> **NOTE**
> If the interfacing does not lie flat, place it under a cutting mat with some weights on it for about 24 hours.

COTTON FABRIC

Make sure to prewash all fabrics before using them, especially dark colors, so that the fabrics don't bleed when they are fused to the interfacing. Similarly, always iron the fabrics before fusing so there are no wrinkles or fold lines. For more information about choosing fabrics, see Chapter 2: Bowl Sizes and Fabrics (page 10).

NONSTICK IRONING SURFACE

Choose a nonstick ironing surface like Goddess Sheet or parchment paper. Make sure that the ironing surface is larger than the piece of interfacing you are working with.

CLEAR TEMPLATE PLASTIC

Clear template plastic is used to create the template pieces needed to create each bowl. Look for sheets 12″ × 18″ (30.5 × 45.7cm).

GENERAL QUILTING AND SEWING SUPPLIES

- Iron
- Ironing board
- Cutting mat 24″ × 36″ (60 × 90cm) or larger
- Quilter's ruler 24″ (60cm) long
- Rotary cutter with a 45mm or 60mm blade
- Blue painter's tape (I like ScotchBlue Original Painter's Tape.)
- Extrafine-tip permanent marker (I like to use a Sharpie.)
- Pencil
- Pins
- Fabric clips
- Seam ripper
- Fabric marker
- Rubber band
- Sewing machine
- Machine sewing needles (sizes 80/12 and 90/14)
- Hand sewing needles (I suggest Quilter's betweens size 9.)
- Threads to match fabric
- Adhesive sand paper fabric grips
- Pressing cloth if using 72F Peltex

chapter 4
TEMPLATES AND INTERFACING

MAKE THE TEMPLATES AND INTERFACING PIECES

Each bowl project will require different templates and interfacing pieces. These instructions give a general guide to creating each template and interfacing piece, but make sure to check the specifics of each project to know exactly which templates to make. See Templates (page 75) for each of the template patterns.

materials

- 1–2 sheets clear template plastic 12″ × 18″ (30.5 × 45.7cm)
- Blue painter's tape
- Extrafine-tip permanent marker (I like to use a Sharpie.)
- Quilter's ruler at least 9″ (23cm)

- Rotary cutter
- Adhesive sandpaper fabric grips
- Heavyweight double-sided fusible interfacing
- Pencil (optional)

MAKE THE TEMPLATES

Because the insides of some of the bowls have many interfacing pieces, it is very important that the templates and interfacing pieces are traced and cut out precisely.

Trace the Templates

1. Secure the template plastic sheet with sandpaper grips so that the plastic does not slide.

2. Cover the pattern with template plastic, and secure it with painter's blue tape.

3. Trace the shape of the pattern onto template plastic with the extrafine-tip permanent marker. Use a ruler to trace the straight lines. Copy all the letters and marks onto the template. This will make it easier to follow the sewing order and to match up the seams when you're creating the bowl. If a template is marked with ½, that means a ½″ (1.2cm) seam allowance has to be added, so make sure to also mark that on the template.

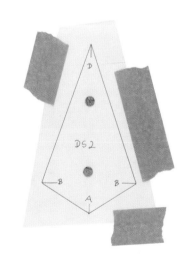

Template plastic secured with blue tape

Cut Out the Template

1. Cut out the template with a rotary cutter. Use a ruler when cutting straight lines, and make sure to cut as precisely as possible. Compare the template to the shape of the template on the book page; they should match exactly.

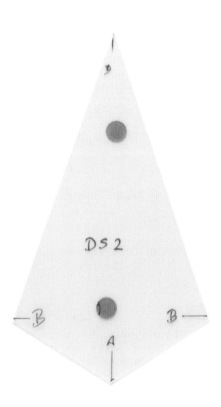

Template cut out

MAKE THE INTERFACING PIECES

Trace the Templates onto Interfacing

1. Place the template onto the interfacing, and secure it with blue tape. Use a pencil or extrafine-tip permanent marker to trace the template onto the interfacing. Copy all the letters and marks, including the dashed lines, onto the interfacing. This will make it easier to follow the sewing order and to match up the seams when you're creating the bowl.

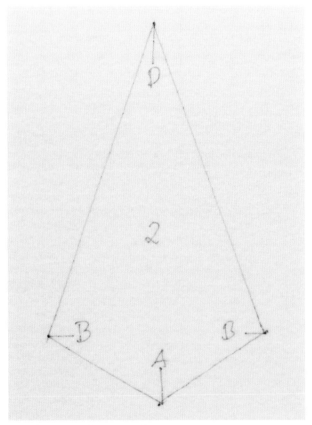

Template traced onto interfacing.

2. With a rotary cutter, cut out the interfacing piece. Always cut just on or inside the traced line. The interfacing piece should fit inside the plastic template piece. This is important if you are working with a heavier fabric that adds bulk to the seams, especially for the Dresden bowl (page 56), which has 18 seams in the inside layer.

TIP *Because heavyweight double-sided fusible interfacing does not give, you can line up two interfacing pieces that share a seam so the points match up.*

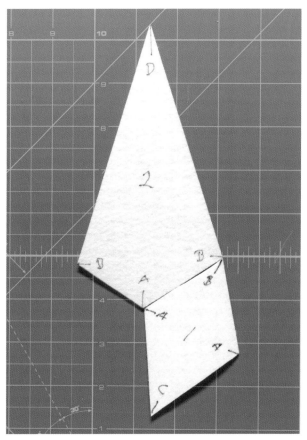

Points A and B matched up

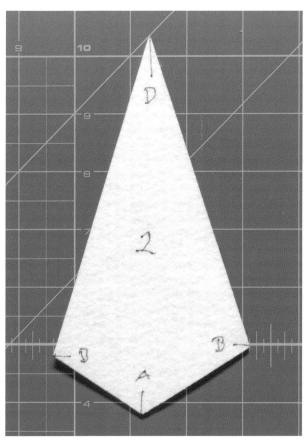

Interfacing piece cut out

chapter 5
BASIC TECHNIQUES FOR ALL BOWLS

The techniques explained in this chapter will appear in almost every bowl project. Use this chapter as a reference guide to refer to as you're making your bowls.

FUSING FABRIC TO HEAVYWEIGHT DOUBLE-SIDED FUSIBLE INTERFACING

1. Cover the ironing board with a nonstick surface such as parchment paper or Goddess Sheet (by mistyfuse.com).

2. Place the interfacing piece on top of the ironing surface with the marks and guidelines facing down. For a reminder about making interfacing pieces, see Chapter 4: Templates and Interfacing (page 20).

3. Cover the interfacing with the fabric, right side facing up. The wrong side of the fabric should be touching the interfacing. Make sure there is enough extra fabric around the interfacing piece for a ½″ (1.2cm) seam allowance on all sides.

4. Fabric will give a little when fused to heavyweight interfacing, so begin by gently pressing the fabric and interfacing together. This will not fuse them together; it will only align them and remove wrinkles. With the iron on the proper setting for the interfacing you are using, slowly start pressing from the center of the piece out toward the edges. Make sure there are no wrinkles. Don't put pressure on the iron as it will leave indentation marks.

5. After the fabric has been pressed to the interfacing, fuse them together following the manufacturer's instructions.

6. Let the piece cool before removing it from the nonstick surface.

Fusing Novelty and Directional Fabrics

It is important that the fabric is placed correctly on the interfacing before the two are fused together.

1. Trace the interfacing piece on a piece of paper, and cut the shape out of the paper. See how this design planning activity works in Chapter 2: Bowl Sizes and Fabrics (page 10).

2. Place the paper on the wrong side of the fabric. Move it around until you find exactly where you want the stripes or motif to appear on the interfacing piece.

Paper placed on wrong side of fabric

TIP *If you are working with striped fabric, mark where the stripes on the fabric should be on the interfacing. Then, line up the marks before fusing to make sure your design will come out as you planned.*

3. Trace the shape onto the wrong side of the fabric with a pencil or fabric marker.

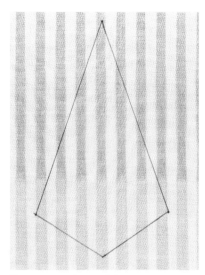

Shape traced onto fabric

4. Place the interfacing piece on the wrong side of the fabric so it fits with the traced line. Tape it in place.

Interfacing piece taped in place

5. Press the interfacing piece to the fabric, then remove the tape and fuse the fabric to the interfacing piece following the interfacing manufacturer's instructions.

TRIMMING FABRIC

These directions are for the inside layer and an outside layer with directional fabric. For an outside layer made with one piece of fabric, see Chapter 6: The Outside Layer (page 34).

After the fabric has been fused to the interfacing, it is trimmed down to allow for a seam allowance.

Trim Straight Edges

1. Trim all sides to ¼″ (6mm) from the edge of the interfacing piece using a quilter's ruler and rotary cutter.

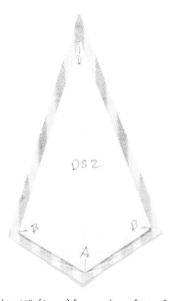

Fabric trimmed to ¼″ (6mm) from edge of interfacing

Trim Curved Edges

If the interfacing piece has a curved edge, it will be a little more difficult to trim the fabric, but precision is just as important.

1. Rubber band a pencil and a light-colored fabric marker together. Make sure the two points are at the same level.

2. Line up one of the points with the edge of the interfacing. If the fabric is dark, run the pencil along the edge of the interfacing and draw a line with the fabric marker. If the fabric is light, run the fabric marker along the edge of the interfacing, and draw a line with the pencil. The line will be approximately ¼″ (6mm) from the edge of the interfacing. If the interfacing edge is marked ½, the seam allowance should be ½″ (1.2cm), so run the line twice.

3. Trim the fabric at the line with a rotary cutter.

Curved seam trimmed

Pencil and fabric marker held together

Trim line drawn; ½″ (1.2cm) line at bottom

SEWING SEAMS

Most of the seams in these projects can be sewn on a machine, and all of them can be sewn by hand.

Straight Seams Sewn on a Machine

1. Line up the pieces you are sewing together so the interfacing pieces are perfectly aligned. If there are points with letters from the template, line up the matching letters.

2. Pin along the edge of the interfacing. Make sure the pins are right along the edge of both the top and bottom pieces.

3. The seam is sewn only along the interfacing, not into the seam allowance. Begin and end the seam with a back stitch. Sew right along the edge of the interfacing. The needle should not go through the interfacing pieces. When the seam is sewn, there should be no gap between the interfacing pieces.

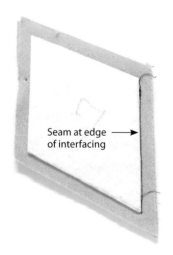

Seam sewn on machine

Seam Allowance Fused to Interfacing Side

Before you can sew some seams, you need to fuse the seam allowance to the interfacing side of the piece.

> **NOTE**
> If you are inserting the center circle by machine, do not fuse the ½″ (1.2cm) seam allowance to the interfacing side. You will need the seam allowance when you insert the center circle.

1. Fold the seam allowance to the interfacing side of the piece with a seam ripper or stiletto. With the tip of an iron, fuse the seam allowance to the interfacing side. For 72F Peltex interfacing, use the wool heat setting on the iron, but do not cover the fabric with a damp cloth.

Fusing seam allowance to interfacing side of piece

2. After the seam allowance is fused, trim down the "rabbit ears" at the tip where two seams meet.

Straight Seams Sewn by Hand

The center star pieces in Bowls 5 and 6 are connected by straight seams that must be sewn by hand.

1. Line up the diamond pieces at Point C.

2. Start hand sewing from Point C, and sew all the way across to Point A. Don't sew into the interfacing. Secure the thread at the beginning and end of the seam with a knot and a double stitch.

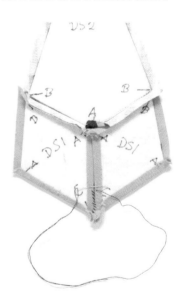

Sewing straight seam by hand

Curved seams

The curved seams can be sewn on a machine or by hand. When sewing on a machine, you may need to adjust the machine's tension. Fuse fabric to two pieces of interfacing with matching edges. Fuse the seam allowance to the interfacing side. Use this as a sample piece to adjust the tension on the sewing machine.

TIP *For concave curves, clip the seam allowance so it lies flat when fused to the interfacing.*

Curved Seams on a Machine

1. Line up the two pieces so the guide lines you drew on the interfacing are aligned. Place the right sides of both pieces up. Use blue tape on the right side of the fabric to hold the two pieces together if necessary.

2. Use a zigzag or decorative stitch to sew the seam from the right side of the pieces. Make sure the needle catches both pieces of interfacing.

Two pieces held together with blue tape

Curved seam sewn on machine

Curved Seams by Hand

1. Line up the two pieces so the guide lines you drew are aligned and the interfacing pieces are flush, interfacing side up. Use blue tape on the interfacing side or pins to hold the two pieces together if necessary.

2. Sew the two pieces together. Don't sew into the interfacing. Secure the thread at the beginning and end of the seam with a knot and a double stitch.

Two pieces held together with blue tape.

Curved seams sewn by hand

INSERTING THE CENTER CIRCLE

Bowls 3 and 4 are based on a pattern with a center circle and six side units. After the side units have been sewn together, they are sewn to the center circle. This can be done by hand or on a machine, depending on the finished look you want for the bowl.

If the center base is sewn by hand, there will be no visible stitching. If the center circle is sewn on a machine, there will be a stitch all along the edge of the center circle.

Sew Center Circle by Hand

When sewing by hand, sew with the interfacing side facing up.

1. Fuse the ½″ (1.2cm) seam allowance to the interfacing side of the center circle (page 28).

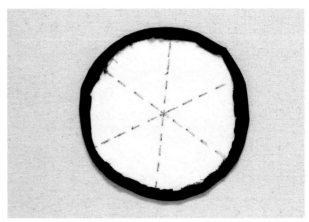

Seam allowance fused to interfacing side

---

2. Place the finished outside layer on the table with the center base facing right side up. Place the inside layer on top with the interfacing facing out. You should be able to see the center base of the outside layer. This will ensure that the inside layer is in the correct place and will make it easier to sew.

Inside layer placed on outside layer

3. Pin the center circle to the sides unit of the inside layer, interfacing facing up. Line up the six guidelines from the center circle with the six seams of the inside layer. The pin needs to catch the fabric on both pieces.

Guide lines and seams aligned and pinned

4. Sew the center circle to the inside layer by hand.

Center circle sewn to six side units (inside layer)

Sew Center Circle on a Machine

The center circle is sewn to the six side units from the fabric side.

1. Fuse the ½″ (1.2cm) seam allowance to the interfacing side of the center circle (page 28).

TIP *Before you sew the last seam, making the six units into a circle, sew a running stitch as a guide along the interfacing edge of the side units. Then sew the last seam.*

2. With the fabric right side up, place the center circle inside the inside layer unit, and press down until it fits. The edge of the center circle should be right at the running stitch.

3. Pin it in place.

Center circle placed inside stitched guide lines and pinned in place

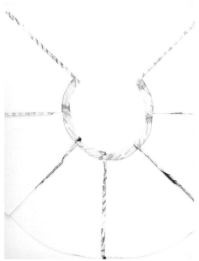

Running stitch sewn along edge of interfacing

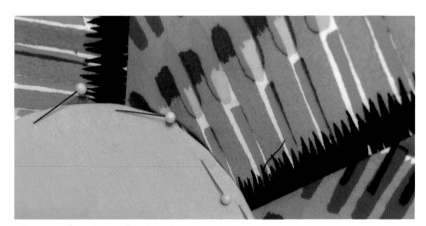

Close-up of center circle pinned

4. Sew the center circle to the ½″ (1.2cm) seam allowance of the inside layer. Stitch right along the edge of the center circle. This stitch will be visible. Remove pins as you sew.

COMPLETING THE BOWL

After the inside layer and outside layer are finished, the two layers are fused together to create the bowl. The edge of the bowl is completed with a bias add-on binding. Bowl 4, the Dresden Bowl with spikes, is not completed with a binding.

TIP *If you are finishing the binding by hand, you should sew on the binding before the two layers are fused together. It is easier to stitch the binding by hand if the two layers are just pressed together, not fused together.*

Combine the Inside and Outside Layers

1. Place the inside layer into the outside layer. Line up the six seams of the outside layer with the six seams of the inside layer, and press down. The inside layer will be about ¼″ (6mm) smaller than the outside layer.

2. Use fabric clips or pins to hold the two layers together.

Inside layer clipped to outside layer

3. The two layers are fused together from the inside of the bowl. The center circle is not fused. Start to fuse from the center of one of the six sides and fuse out toward the seam.

TIP *To determine the time it takes to fuse the layers together, fuse fabric to two leftover pieces of interfacing, noting how much time it takes to fuse the two pieces together. An iron with a higher voltage will fuse faster than an iron with a lower voltage. Keep that in mind as you fuse the layers together.*

Because you are fusing two layers of double fusible interfacing, you might not have to use steam with fast2fuse or a damp cloth with 72F Peltex. Before adding water, try to press the two layers together with the right heat setting for the interfacing you are using.

TIP *It is very important that the heat setting on the iron is correct. If the heat setting is too high, the outside layer interfacing will bubble. If that happens, press it dry from the inside layer with the iron on a lower heat setting.*

Trim the Edge

1. Trim the top edge of the outside layer so it is even with the edge of the fabric of the inside layer.

Add the Binding

materials

- 54″ × 3″ (137.2 × 7.6cm) of bias binding
- 30-weight thread

NOTE ABOUT BINDING

For bowls smaller than the standard pattern, you will need less bias binding. Measure the circumference of the bowl, and add 2½″ (6.4cm).

1. Cut one end of the binding at a 45° angle. Fold ¼″ (6mm) of the end to the wrong side of the fabric, and press.

Folded end of binding

2. Fold the binding in half with long edges together and with the right side of the fabric out. Press.

Binding folded in half

3. Attach the binding to the inside of the bowl with pins or fabric clips. Stretch the binding a bit as you attach it.

4. Sew the binding on by machine, with a ¼″ (6mm) seam allowance. Begin sewing 3½″ (8.9cm) from the tip of the binding. Sew until you reach 1″ (2.5cm) from the tip at the beginning of the binding. Cut off the remaining binding, leaving a 3″ (7.6cm) tail.

5. Tuck the end of the binding into the beginning of the binding, pin, and finish sewing the binding.

End tucked into beginning

6. Pull the folded edge of the binding to the outside of the bowl. Use pins or fabric clips to hold it in place. Pin it to the outside of the bowl.

Binding clipped to outside of bowl

7. Sew the binding to the outside of the bowl either by hand or by machine.

TIP *If you are sewing the binding by machine, sew from the inside of the bowl, and stitch right in the seam of the binding. Hold it in place with fabric clips or pins.*

chapter 6

THE OUTSIDE LAYER

The outside layer is the outside of every finished bowl. The pattern is drawn on heavyweight double-sided fusible interfacing. The interfacing pieces are cut out and then fused to the fabric. The final step is to sew the seams that give the bowl its round shape.

materials

- Heavyweight double-sided fusible interfacing: ⅝ yard (57cm) or one piece 20″ × 20″ (50.8 × 50.8cm)

- Outside fabric: ¾ yard (69cm)

- Clear template plastic

- Quilter's ruler at least 24″ (60cm)

- Rotary cutter

- Blue painter's tape

- Adhesive sandpaper fabric grips

- Fabric clips

- Scissors for cutting paper or plastic

- Extrafine-tip permanent marker (I like to use a Sharpie.)

- Pencil

- 40-weight thread to match fabric

- Machine sewing needle size 70/10 or 80/12

- Pressing cloth (if using 72F Peltex)

cutting

HEAVYWEIGHT DOUBLE-SIDED FUSIBLE INTERFACING:

Cut 1 square 20″ × 20″ (50.8 × 50.8cm).

OUTSIDE FABRIC:

Cut 1 square 20″ × 20″ (50.8 × 50.8cm) for a bowl with binding **OR**

Cut 1 square of fabric 22″ × 22″ (55.9 × 55.9cm) for a bowl without binding.

> **NOTE**
> If the fabric is directional, the design will run in different directions on the six sides.

MAKE THE TEMPLATES

Trace Templates 1 and 2 (pages 78–79) onto template plastic, and cut them out. See Chapter 4: Templates and Interfacing (page 20). Make sure you trace the center lines on Template 1 and mark Point A on Template 2.

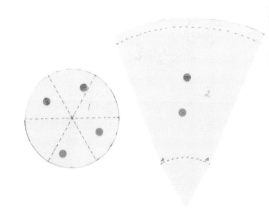

Templates 1 and 2

DRAW THE PATTERN ON THE INTERFACING

The pattern of the bowl is based on a circle. The shape of the bowl is created by cutting out six wedges of the circle.

Draw the Base of the Bowl

1. Draw a dashed line 10″ (25.4cm) in from one of the sides of the interfacing. Mark the midpoint of the dashed line with a ½″ (1.2cm) mark. This marks the center of the interfacing.

2. Place template 1 on the interfacing so the center of the template is on the center of the dashed line.

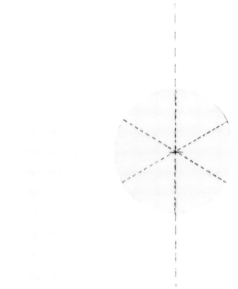

Center dashed line drawn

Template in center of interfacing

---

3. Draw a dashed line around the template. This will be the base of the bowl. Mark the points where the center lines cross the dashed line.

4. Remove the template, and connect the center lines across the circle with dashed lines.

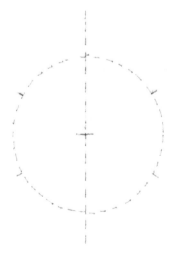

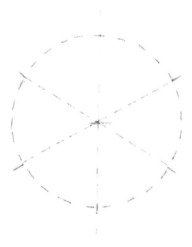

Dashed line around base

All lines marked

5. Place Template 2 on the interfacing so the point of the template is at the center of the base circle and the edges of the template are lined up with the dashed center lines.

6. Draw a solid line around the part of the template not inside the base.

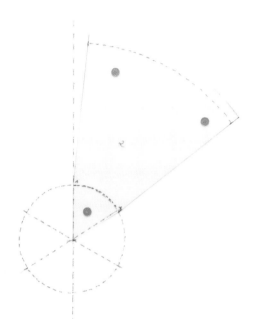

Template lined up with base line

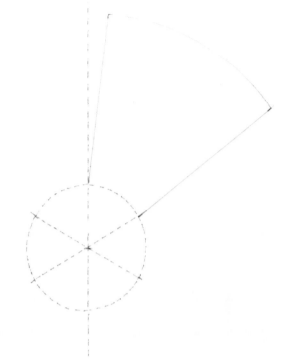

Solid line drawn around template

7. Repeat Steps 6 and 7 until all six sides of the bowl are drawn on the interfacing.

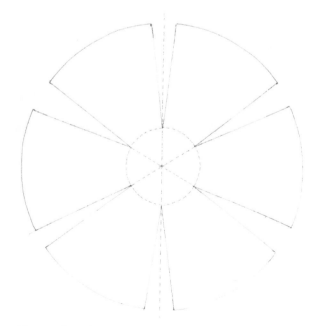

All six wedges drawn

CUT OUT THE INTERFACING

1. Cut out all the **solid** lines with a rotary cutter. Do not cut the dashed lines.

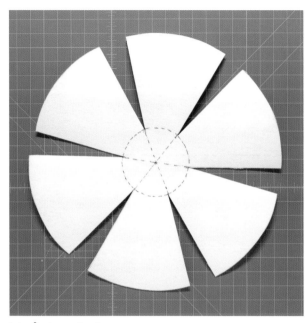

Interfacing cut out

NOTE

For Bowl 4, the Dresden bowl with spikes, trim off ¼″ (6mm) from each of the six curved edges of the interfacing.

FINISH THE OUTSIDE LAYER

1. Fuse the fabric to the interfacing. See Fusing Fabric to Heavyweight Double–Sided Fusible Interfacing (page 25).

NOTE

For Bowl 4, the Dresden bowl with spikes, trim but make sure there is at least ½″ (1.2cm) of extra fabric all the way around the interfacing piece.

2. After the fabric and the interfacing are fused together, trim the fabric down to the outside edge of the interfacing. See Trimming Fabric (page 26). Do not trim inside the six wedges.

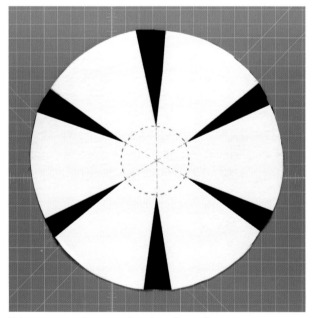

Fabric trimmed to outside edge of interfacing

Score the Fold Lines

1. Use the sharp point of a seam ripper to score the dashed outline of the circle base and the base's center crossing lines on the interfacing. This ensures that the base of the bowl will bend evenly when the seams are sewn.

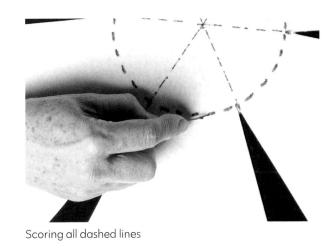

Scoring all dashed lines

Secure the Fabric

1. To ensure that the fabric does not come loose from the interfacing when you turn the outside layer right side out, sew a running stitch on a sewing machine on the dashed line around the center base.

TIP *Pull up the bobbin thread at the beginning and end of the seam so it does not get tangled in the stitches.*

2. Sew a running stitch on a sewing machine ¼″ (6mm) from the edge of the interfacing on both sides of each of the six wedges. This seam will be seen from the outside of the bowl and will help to give the bowl a more finished look. If you do not have a ¼″ foot, draw a line ¼″ (6mm) from the edge of the interfacing to use as a guide.

Start at the top left side of one wedge, and sew down to ¼″ (6mm) past the tip of the wedge. Turn the piece 90°, and sew ¼″ (6mm). Turn the piece 90° again, and sew up the right side of the wedge to the top right corner. Repeat to sew all six wedges.

Running stitch ¼″ (6mm) from edge of interfacing

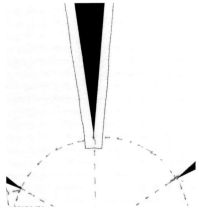

Fabric stitched in place

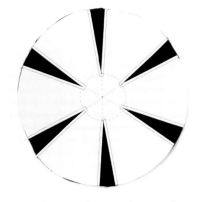

Fabric fused and secured on interfacing

TIP *To ensure an even stich, fuse a small piece of fabric to a small piece of leftover interfacing. Use that piece as a sample to regulate the tension of the sewing machine.*

QUILTING THE OUTSIDE LAYER

If you want to quilt the outside layer, do so at this point, before you sew the corner seams. Note that the fabric between the interfacing wedges of the outside layer will not be seen when the bowl is finished.

SEW THE SEAMS

1. Fold the interfacing and fabric in half along the center line so the fabric is on the inside. Use fabric clips to hold the two sides together.

Outside layer folded

2. Start by sewing the two seams on the bottom folded edge first. Line up the corner tops of the top and bottom interfacing layers.

Pin along the edge of the interfacing so that the point of the pin is facing away from the center. Make sure the pins are right along the edge of both the top and bottom layer of interfacing in order to prevent a gap

when the seams are sewn. Turn the piece around to make sure the pins are running through the fabric along the interfacing edge on the other side.

Seam pinned; front side

3. Sew the seam right along the edge of the interfacing on a machine. Start from the top edge of the interfacing, and sew toward the center. The seam allowance will decrease as you get closer to the base of the bowl. Do a couple of backstitches at the beginning and end of the seam to secure it.

NOTE
For bowls without bindings, start sewing at the edge of the fabric, not the interfacing.

Needle right along edge of interfacing

4. Repeat Steps 2 and 3 until all six seams are sewn.

TRIM AND FINISH

1. With a quilter's ruler and rotary cutter, trim the extra fabric inside the wedges down to ¼″ (6mm) from the edge of the interfacing. You cannot trim all the way down to the base of the bowl, but that's okay.

Seam trimmed

2. Turn the outside layer right side out.

Finished outside layer

TIP *The bases of the inside layers of Bowls 2, 5, and 6 may not lie flat, because the seams meet in the middle. To get an even base, trace Template 1 onto heavyweight interfacing, cut out the interfacing piece, and sew it to the inside of the center base.*

Center base reinforced

MAKE A STURDIER BOWL

The bowls can be made sturdier by adding a layer of nonfusible interfacing between the inside layer and the outside layer. The non-fusible interfacing is fused to the fusible interfacing of the outside layer before the pattern is drawn and cut out. The pattern is drawn on the nonfusible interfacing.

material

- Materials for the outside layer (page 35)
- 1 piece nonfusible heavyweight interfacing
- Presser cloth
- Iron
- Nonstick ironing surface

NOTE
There are two nonfusible heavyweight interfacings on the market: Timtex (by C&T Publishing) and 70 Peltex Sew-In Ultra Firm Stablizer (by Pellon). Both will work for this.

1. Lay down a nonstick ironing surface like parchment paper or Goddess Sheet.

2. Place the fusible interfacing on the nonstick surface, and cover it with the nonfusible interfacing.

3. Cover the nonfusible interfacing with a presser cloth to avoid burn marks on the interfacing. If you are using 72F Peltex, use a damp cloth.

4. With the iron heat setting at the recommended temperature for the interfacing you are using, start fusing the two pieces together. 72F Peltex fuses at wool setting with a damp cloth. fast2fuse uses cotton setting with steam.

Start at the center of the piece, and fuse out to the edges. Because you are fusing through a layer of interfacing, you will have to fuse longer than recommended by the manufacturer. If you want to practice, cut out two small pieces of the interfacings you are working with, and time how long it takes to fuse the two pieces together.

5. Continue to make the outside layer.

chapter 7
CLOTH BOWL– BOWL 1

Bowls made from one piece of cloth are great if you want to show off a beautiful piece of fabric, perhaps something tie-dye, or if you want to add appliqué or embroidery.

materials

- Heavyweight double-sided fusible interfacing: ⅝ yard (57cm) or one piece 20″ × 20″ (50.8 × 50.8cm)

- Inside fabric: ⅝ yard (57cm)

- Clear template plastic

- Quilter's ruler at least 24″ (60cm)

- Rotary cutter

- Blue painter's tape

- Adhesive sandpaper fabric grips

- Scissors for cutting paper or plastic

- Extrafine-tip permanent marker (I like to use a Sharpie.)

- Pencil

- Fabric marker

- Rubber band

- 40-weight thread to match fabric

- Machine sewing needles size 70/10 or 80/12

- Pressing cloth (if using 72F Peltex)

cutting

HEAVYWEIGHT DOUBLE-SIDED FUSIBLE INTERFACING: Cut 1 square of 20″ × 20″ (50.8 × 50.8cm).

INNER FABRIC: Cut 1 square 20″ × 20″ (50.8 × 50.8cm).

templates

For information about creating templates, see Chapter 4: Templates and Interfacing (page 20).

- Template 1, (page 79)

- Template 2, (page 78)

CREATE THE INSIDE LAYER

Prepare the Interfacing

1. Trace Templates 1 and 2 onto the interfacing, following Chapter 6: The Outside Layer, Draw the Base of the Bowl (page 36).

2. Draw a solid line ¼″ (6mm) inside the curved edge of each of the six sides.

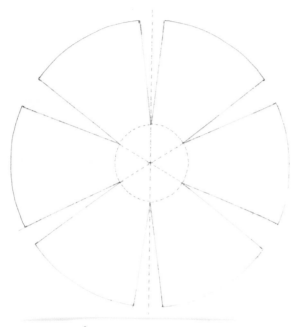

Pattern on interfacing

Solid cutting line drawn

3. Cut out along the **solid** lines with a rotary cutter, trimming ¼″ (6mm) of each outer curve following the new line.

> **NOTE**
> Before you add appliqué fabric or embroidery thread to the bowl, check to make sure it is colorfast so colors do not run when it is fused to the interfacing. Add appliqué or embroidery before fusing the fabric and interfacing. The inside layer can be quilted before or after the seams are sewn. The fabric in the six wedges will not be seen on the finished bowl.

Fuse to Fabric and Trim

1. Fuse the fabric to the interfacing. See Fusing Fabric to Heavyweight Double-Sided Fusible Interfacing (page 25).

2. After the fabric and the interfacing are fused together, trim the fabric to ¼″ (6mm) from the outside edge of the interfacing. See Trimming Fabric (page 26). Do not trim inside the six wedges.

Sew the Seams

To avoid fabric "bubbles" in the center of the bowl, the seams of the inside layer are sewn differently than those of the outside layer.

> **NOTE**
> Do not sew a running stitch to outline the center circle.

1. Fold a wedge with the fabric side in so the tips of the top and bottom interfacing layers are lined up. Pin and sew along the edge of the interfacing. Start sewing the seam ¼″ (6mm) from the center circle. Repeat to sew all six wedges.

Stitching started

2. With a quilter's ruler and rotary cutter, trim the fabric in the six wedges to ¼″ (6mm) from the edge of the interfacing.

The inside layer is now complete.

One-piece inside layer completed

THE OUTSIDE LAYER

1. Refer to Chapter 6: The Outside Layer (page 34) to complete the outside layer.

2. Combine the inside and outside layers, and add a binding by following Completing the Bowl (page 32).

The bowl is now complete.

chapter 8

SIX-PIECE BOWL– BOWL 2

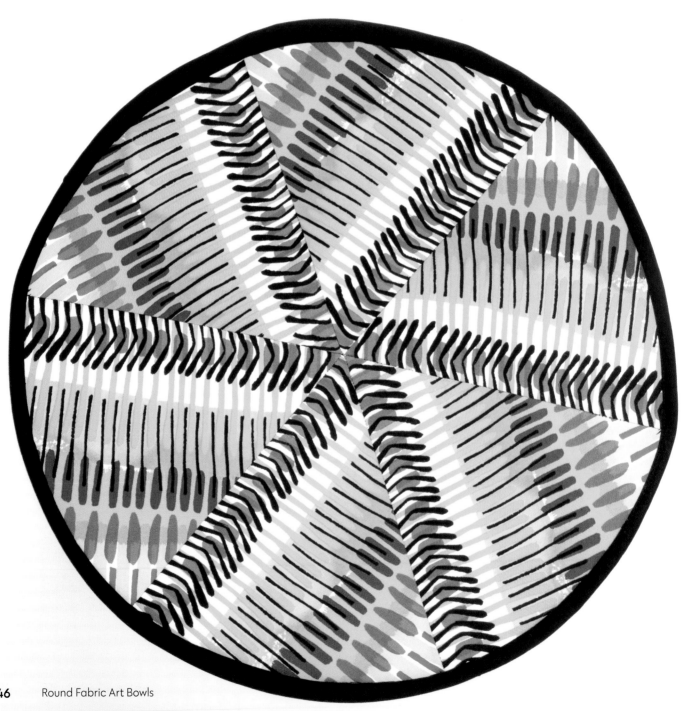

Striped fabrics work great for the six-piece bowl, whether they're oriented vertically, horizontally, or along the seams.

materials

- Heavyweight double-sided fusible interfacing: ⅝ yard (57cm) or one piece 20″ × 20″ (50.8 × 50.8cm)

- Inside fabric: ¾ yard (69cm)

- Clear template plastic

- Quilter's ruler at least 24″ (60cm)

- Rotary cutter

- Blue painter's tape

- Adhesive sandpaper fabric grips

- Scissors for cutting paper or plastic

- Extrafine-tip permanent marker (I like to use a Sharpie.)

- Pencil

- Fabric marker

- Rubber band

- 40-weight thread to match fabric

- Machine sewing needle size 70/10 or 80/12

- Pressing cloth (if using 72F Peltex)

cutting

HEAVYWEIGHT DOUBLE-SIDED FUSIBLE INTERFACING: Cut 1 square 20″ × 20″ (50.8 × 50.8cm).

INSIDE FABRIC: Cut 6 squares 12″ × 12″ (30.5 × 30.5cm).

templates

For information about creating templates, see Chapter 4: Templates and Interfacing (page 20).

- Template 1 (page 79)

- Template 2 (page 78)

> **NOTE ABOUT MATERIALS**
> Depending on the design you choose and the way you want to orient your fabric, you may need more fabric.

THE INSIDE LAYER

Prepare the Interfacing

1. Trace around Templates 1 and 2 onto the interfacing, following Chapter 6: The Outside Layer, Draw the Base of the Bowl (page 36).

2. Change the dashed lines inside the center circle to solid lines. Leave the center circle itself dashed.

3. Draw a solid line ¼″ (6mm) from the outer edge of each wedge. This is the new cutting line. Number the wedges 1 through 6.

4. With a Quilter's ruler and rotary cutter, cut on all the **solid** lines. Do not cut the dashed lines.

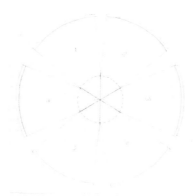

Altered pattern

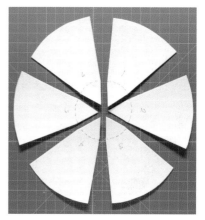

Six wedges cut out

Fuse to Fabric and Trim

1. Fuse the fabric to each piece of interfacing. See Fusing Fabric to Heavyweight Double-Sided Fusible Interfacing (page 25).

2. After the fabric and the interfacing are fused together, trim the fabric to ¼″ (6mm) from the outside edge of the interfacing of each wedge. See Trimming Fabric (page 26).

Interfacing wedges fused and trimmed

Sew the Seams

1. Place Wedge 2 on top of Wedge 1, fabric sides together, and pin at the tip. Line up the dashed lines on both wedges, and pin again. Then pin the rest of the seam right along the edge of the interfacing.

Pieces 1 and 2 pinned

2. Sew the two wedges together. Make sure they remain lined up at the point and along the dashed line.

3. Repeat Steps 1 and 2 to sew Wedges 2 and 3 together. Sew the seam with Wedge 3 on top.

One-half of inside layer, interfacing side

One-half of inside layer, fabric side

4. Repeat Steps 1–3 to attach Wedges 4, 5, and 6. You now have both halves of the inside layer.

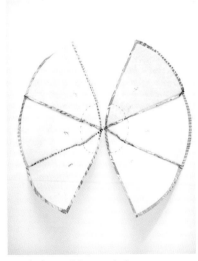

Two halves of the inside layer

5. Line up the two halves, fabric sides together, and pin at the center point. Then pin out toward the dashed lines on both sides of the center point. Make sure the center point and dashed lines are lined up.

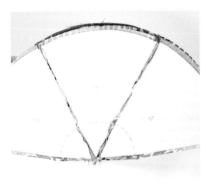

Center point and up to dashed line pinned

6. Sew from the first dashed line, through the center point, to the second dashed line. The center point is now secured. Sew from the dashed line out to the edge of the interfacing on both sides.

Inside layer finished

THE OUTSIDE LAYER

1. Refer to Chapter 6: The Outside Layer (page 34) to complete the outside layer.

2. Combine the inside and outside layers, and add a binding by following Completing the Bowl (page 32).

The bowl is now complete.

Six piece bowl in red, black, and gold

VARIATION

Each piece of the six-piece bowl can be made of several fabrics. To do this, the interfacing pieces need to be cut into several pieces. Make template pieces, and trace them onto the interfacing as normal. Then cut the interfacing pieces into strips. Do not cut the strips thinner than 1″ (2.5cm) wide. Fuse and trim the fabric like normal. Then combine the pieces back into six units by sewing them together.

Interfacing cut into 2″ (5.1cm) strips

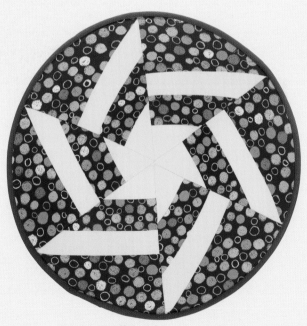

Bowl with different fabrics in each unit

chapter 9

FLOWER BOWL– BOWL 3

Round Fabric Art Bowls

Scraps work great for this bowl! Use different fabrics for each petal to add interest and uniqueness to your design.

materials

- Heavyweight double-sided fusible interfacing: ⅝ yard (57cm) or one piece 20″ × 20″ (50.8 × 50.8cm)

- Inside fabric:

  Petal FB1: ¼ yard or 1 fat quarter (23cm)

  Petal FB3: ¼ yard or 1 fat quarter (23cm)

  Background FB2: ¼ yard or 1 fat quarter (23cm)

  Center circle: 1 square 6″ × 6″ (15.2 × 15.2cm)

- Clear template plastic

- Quilter's ruler at least 24″ (60cm)

- Rotary cutter

- Blue painter's tape

- Adhesive sandpaper fabric grips

- Scissors for cutting paper or plastic

- Extrafine-tip permanent marker (I like to use a Sharpie.)

- Pencil

- Fabric marker

- Rubber band

- 40-weight thread to match fabric

- Machine sewing needles size 70/10 or 80/12

- Pressing cloth (if using 72F Peltex)

cutting

HEAVYWEIGHT DOUBLE-SIDED FUSIBLE INTERFACING: Cut 1 square 20″ × 20″ (50.8 × 50.8cm).

INSIDE FABRIC: See instructions below for cutting individual shapes.

templates

For information about creating templates, see Chapter 4: Templates and Interfacing (page 20).

- Template FB1 (page 77)

- Template FB2 (page 77)

- Template FB3 (page 77)

- Center Circle (Template 1) (page 79)

NOTE ABOUT MATERIALS

If you want each petal in this bowl to be made of the same fabric, use the same fabric for FB1 and FB3. All measurements are for fabrics without directional patterns. If your design incorporates orienting directional fabric in different ways, you may need additional fabric.

Use Pattern 1 to create the center circle template. FB1 and FB3 each make up half of a petal. FB1, FB2, and FB3 should be drawn onto template plastic as one unit and then cut into three pieces.

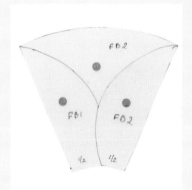

Templates FB1, FB2, and FB3 as one unit

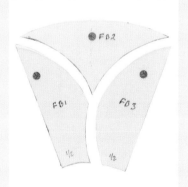

Templates FB1, FB2, and FB3 cut out

THE INSIDE LAYER

This bowl consists of six side units and a center circle. Each side unit is made up of three separate pieces that create the petal shape.

Draw the Pattern on Interfacing

1. Trace the center circle using Template 1 onto interfacing with a solid line. Draw the six center lines with dashed lines. Cut out on the solid line. See Make the Interfacing Pieces in Chapter 4: Templates and Interfacing (page 20).

2. Tape Templates FB1, FB2, and FB3 together with blue tape, and then trace them onto the interfacing as one unit.

3. Remove Template FB1, and draw a line along the edge of FB2 and FB3.

Center circle cut out of interfacing

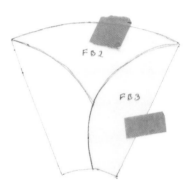

Templates FB1, FB2, and FB3 as one unit

Template FB1 removed

4. Remove Template FB2 and draw a line along the edge of FB3.

5. Repeat Steps 2–4 to create six total units. Number each unit 1 through 6.

FB2 removed

One unit in interfacing

6. Draw a couple of horizontal guide lines across the seam lines of each piece. These will help to align them perfectly when you sew them together later.

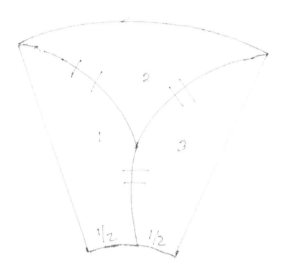

Interfacing pieces with alignment lines

7. Cut out each unit.

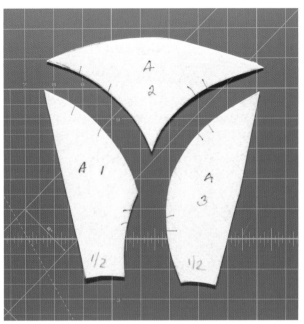

Individual pieces numbered and cut out (1 for FB1, 2 for FB2, and 3 for FB3)

TIP *Keep the pieces for each petal separate in small bags, or hold them together with a fabric clip. You also can give each piece in the unit a letter so you know which pieces go together.*

Fuse to Fabric and Trim

1. Fuse the fabric to each piece of interfacing. See Fusing Fabric to Heavyweight Double-Sided Fusible Interfacing (page 25).

2. After the fabric and the interfacing are fused together, trim the fabric. See Trimming Fabric (page 26).

3. For curved edges, fuse the seam allowance to the interfacing. See Seam Allowance Fused to Interfacing Side (page 28). On Pieces 1 and 3, fuse the curved seam allowance to the interfacing side except the side marked ½. On Piece 2, fuse the curved seam allowance to the interfacing side except the top seam allowance.

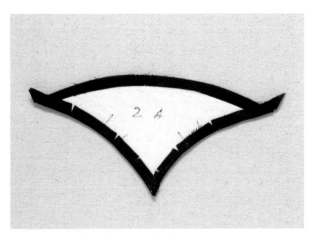

Piece 2 with only side seams fused

Sew the Units Together

These seams can be sewn by hand or machine. Machine-sewn seams should be sewn on the fabric side with a zigzag or decorative stitch. It's very important to follow the right sewing order for this bowl.

1. Sew Piece 1 to Piece 2.

Pieces 1 and 2 sewn together, interfacing side

Pieces 1 and 2 sewn together, fabric side

2. Sew Piece 3 to Pieces 1 and 2 to create one unit.

Piece 3 sewn to Pieces 1 and 2, interfacing side

Piece 3 sewn to Pieces 1 and 2, fabric side

3. Repeat Steps 4 and 5 to create six units.

4. If you are inserting the center circle by hand, sew all six units together along the long edges to make a circle. Backstitch at the beginning and end of each seam. If you are inserting the center circle by machine, sew the units into one piece, but not into a circle.

Six units sewn together

Center Circle

Insert the center circle by hand or on a machine. See Inserting the Center Circle (page 30). The inside layer of the bowl is now finished.

NOTE

If you want to insert the center circle by hand, fuse the ½″ (1.2cm) seam allowance to the wrong side of the interfacing at this point.

Finished inside layer of flower bowl

THE OUTSIDE LAYER

1. Refer to Chapter 6: The Outside Layer (page 34) to complete the outside layer.

2. Combine the inside and outside layers, and add a binding by following Completing the Bowl (page 32).

The bowl is now complete.

VARIATION

The six side units do not have to be made into petals. Each unit can be made of just one piece of interfacing.

Flower bowl variation

chapter 10
DRESDEN BOWL– BOWL 4

The Dresden bowl consists of eighteen pieces with spikes projecting from the center circle. You can split the spikes in half for a more complex design. You also can remove the spikes for a simpler design. Contrasting colors, like black and white, work great for this bowl.

materials

- Heavyweight double-sided fusible interfacing: ¾ yard (69cm) or one piece 20″ × 20″ (50.8 × 50.8cm)

- Inside fabric:

  Spikes: ¾ yard (69cm) **or**

  For two-color spikes: ½ yard (46cm) each of 2 fabrics

  Spike backing: ⅜ yard (34cm)

  Center circle: 6″ × 6″ (15 × 15cm)

- Clear template plastic

- Quilter's ruler at least 24″ (60cm)

- Rotary cutter

- Blue painter's tape

- Adhesive sandpaper fabric grips

- Scissors for cutting paper or plastic

- Extrafine-tip permanent marker (I like to use a Sharpie.)

- Pencil

- Fabric marker

- Rubber band

- Seam ripper

- 40-weight thread to match fabric

- Machine sewing needles size 70/10 or 80/12

- Pressing cloth (if using 72F Peltex)

cutting

HEAVYWEIGHT DOUBLE-SIDED FUSIBLE INTERFACING

Cut 1 rectangle 24″ × 20″ (61 × 50.8cm) **OR**

Cut 36 rectangles 3½″ × 9″ (8.9 × 22.9cm).

Cut 1 square 5½″ × 5½″ (14 × 14cm).

INSIDE FABRIC

Cut 18 rectangles 10″ × 3¾″ (25.4 × 9.5cm) for spikes *or*

Cut 18 rectangles 10″ × 2⅕″ (25.4 × 6.4cm) from each of 2 fabrics for two-color spikes.

Cut 18 rectangles 3½″ × 4″ (8.9 × 10.2cm) for spike backing.

Cut 1 square 6″ × 6″ (15.2 × 15.2cm) for center circle.

templates

For information about creating templates, see Chapter 4: Templates and Interfacing (page 20).

- Template DS (page 75)

- Center Circle (Template 1) (page 79)

NOTE ABOUT MATERIALS

All measurements are for fabrics without directional patterns. If your design incorporates orienting directional fabric in different ways, you may need additional fabric.

Use Template 1 to create the center circle. Make sure to mark the letters and midpoint marks on Template DS. If you are making split spikes, after Step 3, cut each spike in half at the midpoint mark to create 36 half spikes. Mark each left half spike with a 1, and each right half spike with a 2.

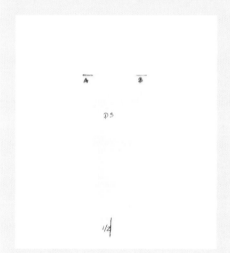

Template DS

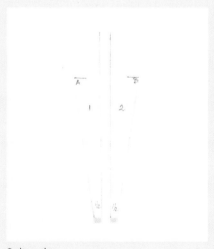

Split spike

THE INSIDE LAYER

Draw the Pattern on Interfacing

1. Trace the center circle using Template 1 onto interfacing with a solid line. Draw the six center lines with dashed lines. Cut out on the solid line. See Chapter 4: Templates and Interfacing, Make the Interfacing Pieces (page 22).

2. Trace eighteen pieces of Template DS onto interfacing.

3. Cut out all the **solid** lines with a rotary cutter. Do not cut the dashed lines. Cut right inside the line of each piece, never outside the line.

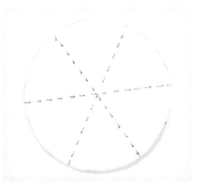

Center circle cut out of interfacing

Fuse to Fabric and Trim

1. Fuse the fabric to each piece of interfacing. See Fusing Fabric to Heavyweight Double-Sided Fusible Interfacing (page 25).

2. After the fabric and the interfacing are fused together, trim the fabric to ¼″ (6mm) from the outside edge of the interfacing. If the interfacing is marked ½, trim the fabric to ½″ (1.2cm). See Trimming Fabric (page 26).

Sew Split Spikes

If you created split spikes, sew each pair together into one spike.

Two split halves sewn together into one spike, interfacing side

Back the Spikes

1. Line up the backing fabric with the interfacing piece, right sides together. Make sure the backing extends at least ½″ (1.2cm) beyond Points A and B.

Backing fabric for spikes lined up

2. Start sewing at Point A, backstitch, then continue to the top of the spike, including the seam allowance. Sew from the seam allowance at the top of the spike down to Point B. Back stitch at Point B.

Backing fabric sewn to spike

3. Trim the fabric to ¼″ (6mm) from the sides of the spike and ⅛″ (3mm) from the top of the spike.

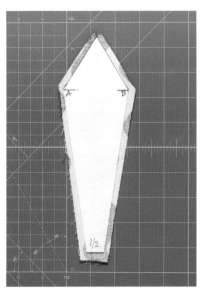

Backing sewn and trimmed

4. Turn the backing fabric right side out. Use a seam ripper to gently pull out at the point if necessary. To make it easier to sew the pieces in the next step, draw the ¼″ (6mm) sewing line on the backing fabric.

Backing fabric turned right side out, with sewing lines

5. Repeat Steps 1–4 to add backing to each spike.

Sew the Seams

1. Place two spikes together, and sew from the base up to Point A. Backstitch at the beginning and end of the seam.

Two pieces sewn together

2. Sew a third spike onto the first two to create a unit.

3. Repeat Steps 1 and 2 to create three units.

> **NOTE**
>
> If you are inserting the center circle by hand, fuse the ½″ (1.2cm) seam allowance onto the interfacing side of each unit. See Seam Allowance Fused to Interfacing Side in Chapter 5: Basic Techniques for All Bowls (page 24).

4. If you are inserting the center circle by hand, sew all six units together along the long edges to make a circle. Backstitch at the beginning and end of each seam. If you are inserting the center circle by machine, sew the units into one piece, but not into a circle.

All six units sewn together

Center Circle

1. Insert the center circle by hand or on a machine. See Inserting the Center Circle (page 30). The inside layer of the bowl is now finished.

Inside layer finished

THE OUTSIDE LAYER

This bowl has alterations to the outside layer.

1. Follow Chapter 6: The Outside Layer (page 34) through Cut Out the Interfacing to prepare the interfacing.

2. Trim ¼″ (6mm) off the outer edge of each of the six outside edges.

3. Fuse the fabric to the interfacing. See Fusing Fabric to Heavyweight Double-Sided Fusible Interfacing (page 25). Then, trim ½″ (1.2cm) from the edge of the interfacing of each piece.

4. Refer to Chapter 6: The Outside Layer, Score the Fold Lines (page 39), and follow through Sew the Seams to sew the outside layer.

5. Fuse the ½″ (1.2cm) seam allowance to the interfacing side. See Seam Allowance Fused to Interfacing Side in Chapter 5: Basic Techniques for All Bowls (page 28).

---

6. Turn the outside layer right side out.

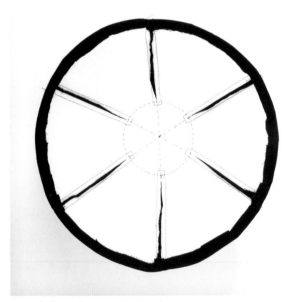

Outside layer for Dresden bowl

7. Combine the inside and outside layers by following Completing the Bowl (page 32). The Dresden bowl with spikes does not have a binding. To complete the bowl, hand stitch the edge of the outer layer to the spikes of the inside layer.

Finished edge

The bowl is now complete.

VARIATION

To make this bowl without the spikes, alter the template. Cut the tip of the spike off the DS template from Point A to Point B. Complete the inside layer as instructed in this chapter. Then follow the standard directions for creating the outside layer, and add a binding.

Altered template

Dresden bowl without spikes

chapter 11

SINGLE-STAR BOWL—BOWL 5

The pattern for the single-star bowl is based on a six-pointed star, and the bowl can easily be made in a day. The seams of the center star are sewn by hand.

materials

- Heavyweight double-sided fusible interfacing: ⅝ yard or one piece 20″ × 20″ (50.8 × 50.8cm)
- Inside fabric:

  For Shape S1: ¼ yard or a fat quarter (23cm)

  For Shape S2: ¼ yard or a fat quarter (23cm)
- Clear template plastic
- Quilter's ruler at least 24″ (60cm)
- Rotary cutter
- Blue painter's tape
- Adhesive sandpaper fabric grips
- Scissors for cutting paper or plastic
- Extrafine-tip permanent marker (I like to use a Sharpie.)
- Pencil
- Fabric marker
- Rubber band
- 40-weight thread to match fabric
- Machine sewing needles size 70/10 or 80/12
- Pressing cloth (if using 72F Peltex)

cutting

Heavyweight double-sided fusible interfacing:

Cut 1 square 20″ × 20″ (50.8 × 50.8cm).

Inside fabric:

See instructions below for cutting individual shapes.

templates

For information about creating templates, see Chapter 4: Templates and Interfacing (page 20).

- Template S1 (page 75)
- Template S2 (page 76)

NOTE ABOUT MATERIALS

All measurements are for fabrics without directional patterns. If your design incorporates orienting directional fabric in different ways, you may need additional fabric.

Templates S1 and S2

THE INSIDE LAYER

Draw the Pattern on Interfacing

1. Make six S1 interfacing pieces and six S2 interfacing pieces following Chapter 4: Templates and Interfacing, Make the Interfacing Pieces (page 22).

2. Mark each interfacing piece with a number (1 for S1 and 2 for S2).

Fuse to Fabric and Trim

1. Fuse the fabric to each piece of interfacing. See Fusing Fabric to Heavyweight Double-Sided Fusible Interfacing (page 25).

2. After the fabric and the interfacing are fused together, trim the fabric to ¼″ (6mm) from the outside edge of the interfacing of each piece. See Trimming Fabric (page 26).

3. On Piece 1, fuse the seam allowance to the interfacing side from the center point to Point A. See Seam Allowance Fused to Interfacing Side (page 28).

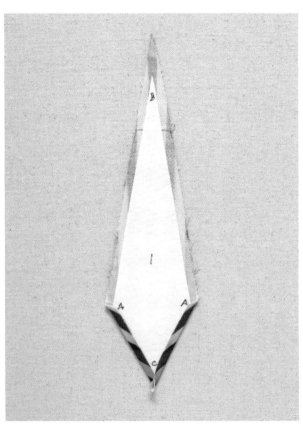

Seam allowances at center point fused to back side of interfacing on Piece 1, center star

Sew the Seams

1. Line up Point A on Piece 1 with Point A on Piece 2. Because the seam allowance of the center star point is fused to the back side of the interfacing, the seam starts ¼″ (6mm) from the seam allowance of Piece 2.

Piece 1 and Piece 2 lined up

2. Pin and sew the two pieces together from Point A to Point B. This is one unit.

3. Repeat Steps 1 and 2 to make six units.

4. Line up two units so Point A and Point B of one unit are lined up with Point A and Point B of the second unit. Pin and sew from Point A to Point B.

Two units lined up

Two units sewn together

5. Combine all six units so they make a circle. The seams of the center star are not sewn yet.

All six units sewn together

Center Star Seams

1. Sew the center star seams by hand. See Straight Seams by Hand (page 28). It's easiest to sew from Point C, at the tip, to Point A. The inside layer is now finished.

Finished inside layer

THE OUTSIDE LAYER

1. Refer to Chapter 6: The Outside Layer (page 34) to complete the outside layer.

2. Combine the inside and outside layers, and add a binding by following Completing the Bowl (page 32).

The bowl is now complete.

chapter 12
DOUBLE-STAR BOWL—BOWL 6

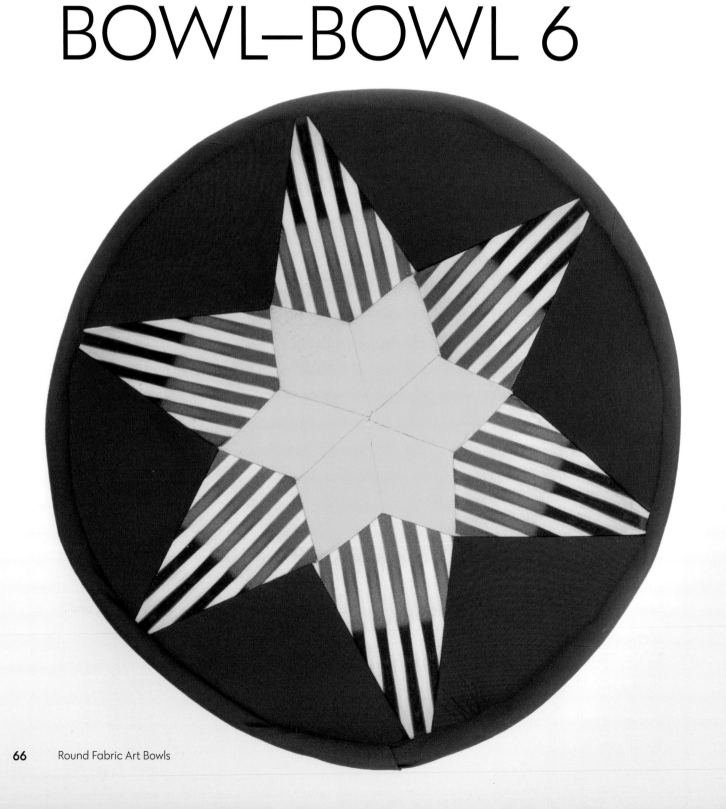

The pattern for the double-star bowl is based on a six-pointed star, just like the single-star bowl. But a second star is added to the design for additional interest. The seams of the center star are sewn by hand. Scraps work great for this bowl.

materials

- Heavyweight double-sided fusible interfacing: ⅝ yard or one piece 20″ × 20″ (50.8 × 50.8cm)

- Inside fabric:

  For Shape DS1: ¼ yard or a fat quarter (23cm)

  For Shape DS2: ¼ yard or a fat quarter (23cm)

  For Shape DS3: ⅓ yard or a fat quarter (31cm)

- Clear template plastic

- Quilter's ruler at least 24″ (60cm)

- Rotary cutter

- Blue painter's tape

- Adhesive sandpaper fabric grips

- Scissors for cutting paper or plastic

- Extrafine-tip permanent marker (I like to use a Sharpie.)

- Pencil

- Fabric marker

- Rubber band

- 40-weight thread to match fabric

- Machine sewing needle size 70/10 or 80/12

- Pressing cloth (if using 72F Peltex)

cutting

Heavyweight double-sided fusible interfacing:

Cut 1 square 20″ × 20″ (50.8 × 50.8cm).

Inside fabric:

See instructions below for cutting individual shapes.

templates

For information about creating templates, see Chapter 4: Templates and Interfacing (page 20).

- Template DS1 (page 75)

- Template DS2 (page 76)

- Template DS3 (page 79)

NOTE ABOUT MATERIALS

All measurements are for fabrics without directional patterns. If your design incorporates orienting directional fabric in different ways, you may need additional fabric.

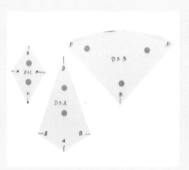

DS1, DS2, and DS3 templates with markings

THE INSIDE LAYER

Draw the Pattern on Interfacing

1. Make six DS1 interfacing pieces, six DS2 interfacing pieces, and six DS3 interfacing pieces following Make the Interfacing Pieces (page 22).

2. Mark each interfacing piece with a number (1 for DS1, 2 for DS2, and 3 for DS3).

Fuse to Fabric and Trim

1. Fuse the fabric to each piece of interfacing. See Fusing Fabric to Heavyweight Double–Sided Fusible Interfacing (page 25).

2. After the fabric and the interfacing are fused together, trim the fabric down to ¼″ (6mm) from the outside edge of the interfacing of each piece. See Trimming Fabric (page 26).

3. On Piece 1, fuse the seam allowance to the interfacing side from Point C to Point A. See Seam Allowance Fused to Interfacing Side (page 28).

Sew the Seams

1. Line up Point A on Piece 1 with Point A on Piece 2. Because the seam allowance of the center star point is fused to the back side of the interfacing, the seam starts ¼″ (6mm) from the seam allowance of Piece 2.

2. Pin and sew the two pieces together from Point A to Point B. This is one unit.

3. Repeat Steps 1 and 2 to make six units.

4. Sew a piece 3 to each unit. Line up Pieces 2 and 3, and sew from Point D to Point B.

Pin and sew from Point D to Point B

Piece 1 and Piece 2 sewn together, interfacing side

Piece 1 and Piece 2 lined up

Pieces 1 and 2 sewn together, fabric side

Sew Units Together

1. Sew all the units together. Seam 1: Line up Piece 1 from one unit and Piece 2 from a second unit. Sew from Point B to Point A.

Two units lined up

Pin and sew from Point B to Point A.

2. Seam 2: Sew Pieces 2 and 3 together with Piece 3 on top. Do not pin. Start at Point B, and use your hand to pull the two pieces together so that the edges of the seam allowances on Piece 2 and Piece 3 line up. Sew slowly on a machine.

Starting at point B

Two units sewn together

3. Repeat Steps 1 and 2 to sew all six units together into a circle. The seams of the center star are not sewn yet.

All six units sewn together

Center Star Seams

1. Sew the center star seams by hand. See Straight Seams by Hand (page 28). It's easiest to sew from Point C, at the tip, to Point A. The inside layer is now finished.

Finished inside layer

THE OUTSIDE LAYER

1. Refer to Chapter 6: The Outside Layer (page 34) to complete the outside layer.

2. Combine the inside and outside layers, and add a binding by following Completing the Bowl (page 32).

The bowl is now complete.

chapter 13
CHANGING THE SIZE OF THE BOWL

DECIDE ON THE BOWL SIZE

The patterns in this book are based on a bowl with a center circle radius of 2½″ (6.4cm) and an outer circle with a radius of 9″ (22.9cm). So all inside layer templates will fit only in a bowl that size. Bowl 1 and Bowl 2 can be made smaller using Templates 1 and 2 to change the radius of both the center circle and the outer circle.

NOTE
If you want a specific motif in the center of the bowl, measure the diameter of the motif, and divide it by 2. That should be the radius of the center circle to fit your motif.

SUGGESTED SIZES FOR SMALLER BOWLS

Center circle radius 1″ (2.5cm); outer circle radius 2½″ (6.4cm)

Center circle radius 2″ (5.1cm); outer circle radius 4″ (10.2cm)

Center circle radius 2½″ (6.4cm); outer circle radius 6½″ (16.5cm)

materials

- 2 squares of heavyweight double-sided fusible interfacing based on the chosen size of the bowl
- Fabric to cover interfacing and create binding based on the chosen size of the bowl
- Quilter's ruler at least 24″ (60cm)
- Rotary cutter
- Scissors for cutting paper or plastic
- Pencil
- Fabric marker
- Rubber band
- Tool to draw circles, like a compass

Templates:

- Template 1 (page 79)
- Template 2 (page 78)

NOTE ABOUT MATERIALS
The length of the binding will be the circumference of the outside circle plus 3″ (7.6cm).

PREPARE THE INTERFACING

To calculate the size of the interfacing you need, multiply the radius of the outer circle (from the center to the outer edge) by 2, then add 1″ (2.5cm). So if the radius of the outer circle is 4″ (10.2cm), the interfacing square should be 9″ × 9″ (22.9 × 22.9cm).

$$(4″ × 2 = 8″) + 1″ = 9″$$

$$(10.2cm × 2 = 20.4cm) + 2.5cm = 22.9cm$$

The patterns for interfacing pieces for the outside layer and inside layer are drawn at the same time. Mark the inside layer **IL,** and mark the outside layer **OL.**

1. Mark the midpoint on each of the two interfacing pieces. Line up Template 1 so the center of the template is at the midpoint. Mark the six separate 60° angle points around the midpoint to divide the space into six equal angles.

2. Connect the six angle points to the center with a dashed line.

Angle points connect

Six marked 60° angle points

3. With a dashed line, draw the center circle using a compass or similar tool. Make sure you draw the center circle on both pieces of interfacing before you change the radius of the compass for the outside circle.

4. On the interfacing piece marked **IL**, draw the outside circle with a solid line.

Inside layer with solid line outer circle drawn

5. On the interfacing piece marked **OL**, draw the outside circle with a dashed line. Then measure ¼″ (6mm) from the dashed line, and draw a solid line around the circle.

Outside layer drawn with ¼″ (6mm) added

Center circle drawn

---

6. Place Template 2 so the left side of the template is lined up with the left side of one of the dashed center lines and Point A is lined up wih the dashed line of the center circle. Draw a solid line along the side of the template from Point A to the outer circle.

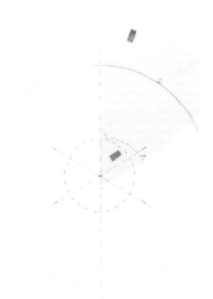

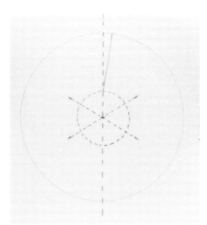

Solid line

Template 2 lined up, left side

7. Repeat step 6 for the right side.

8. Repeat Steps 6 and 7 for all six angles.

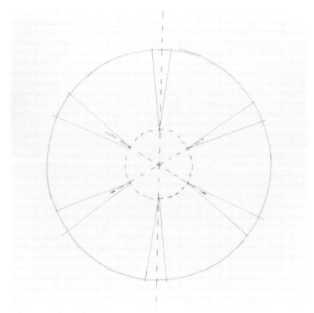

All six wedges drawn

9. Repeat Steps 6–8 for the inside layer piece.

10. With a rotary cutter, cut out the interfacing piece on the **solid** lines. You can now follow the instructions in Chapter 7: Cloth Bowl—Bowl 1 to complete a bowl in a new size.

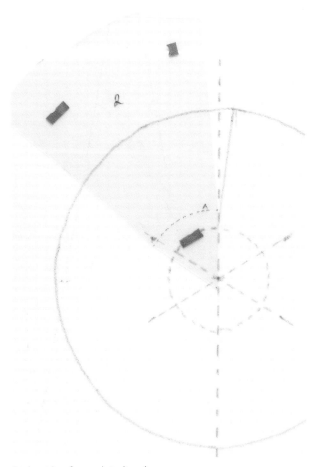

Right side of template lined up

Wedge drawn

TEMPLATES

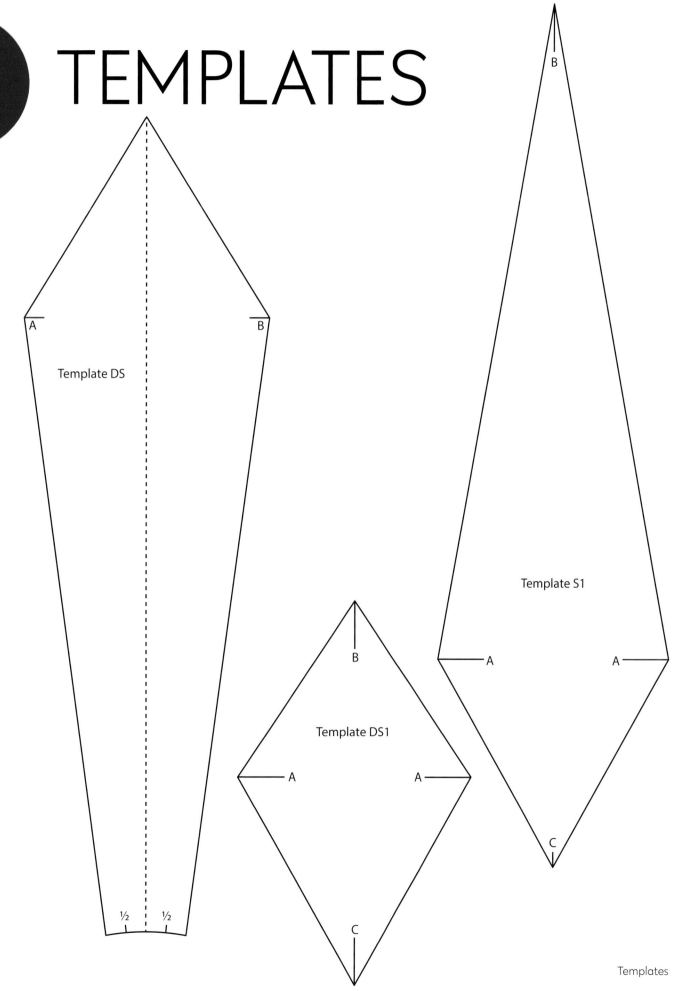

Template DS

½ ½

Template DS1

B

A A

C

Template S1

B

A A

C

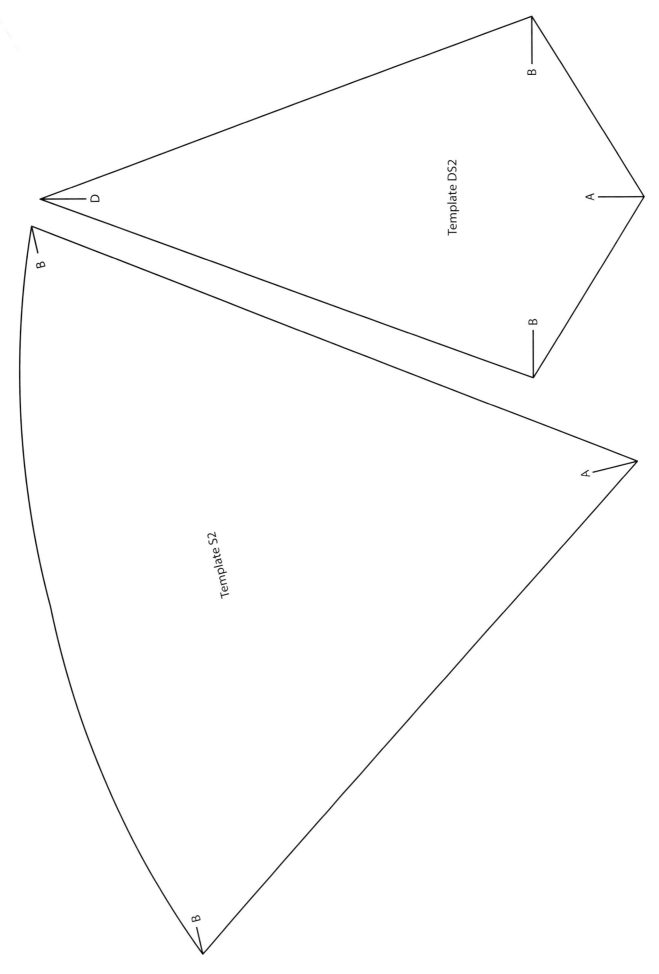

Template DS2

Template S2

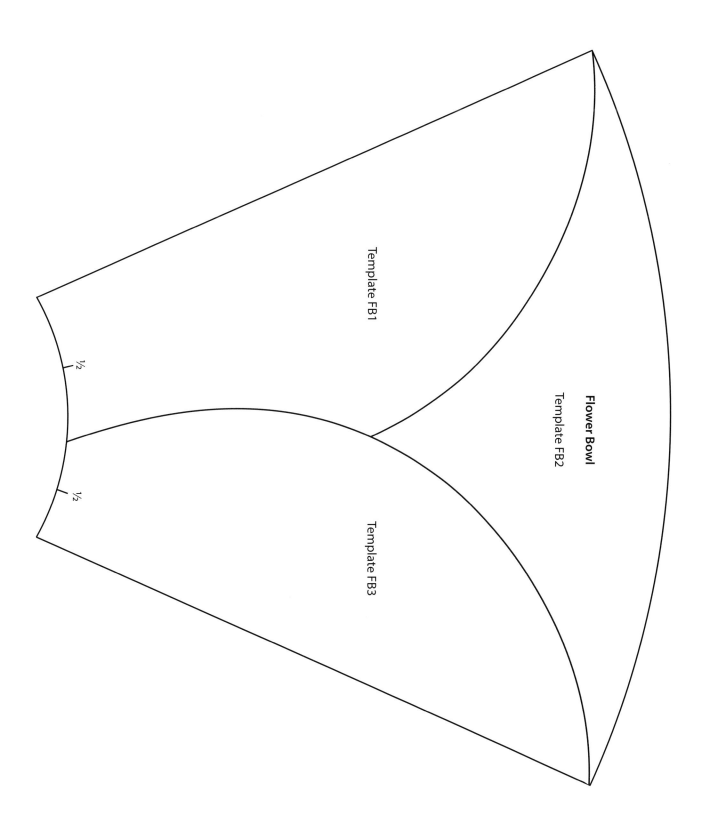

Template FB1

Flower Bowl
Template FB2

Template FB3

½

½

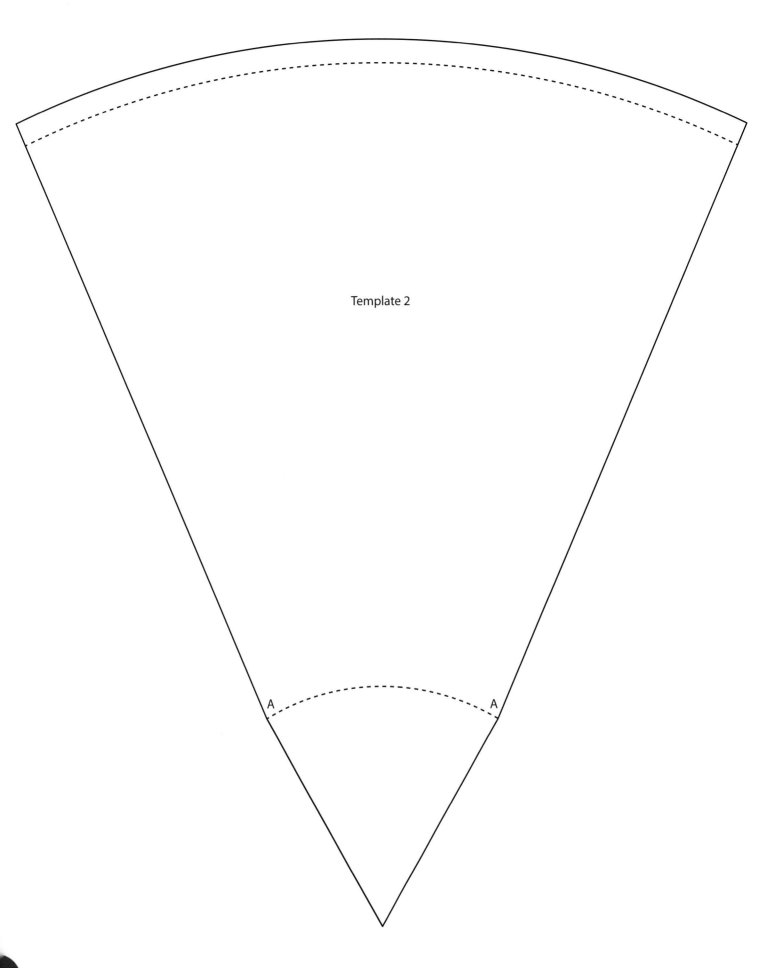

Template 2

A   A

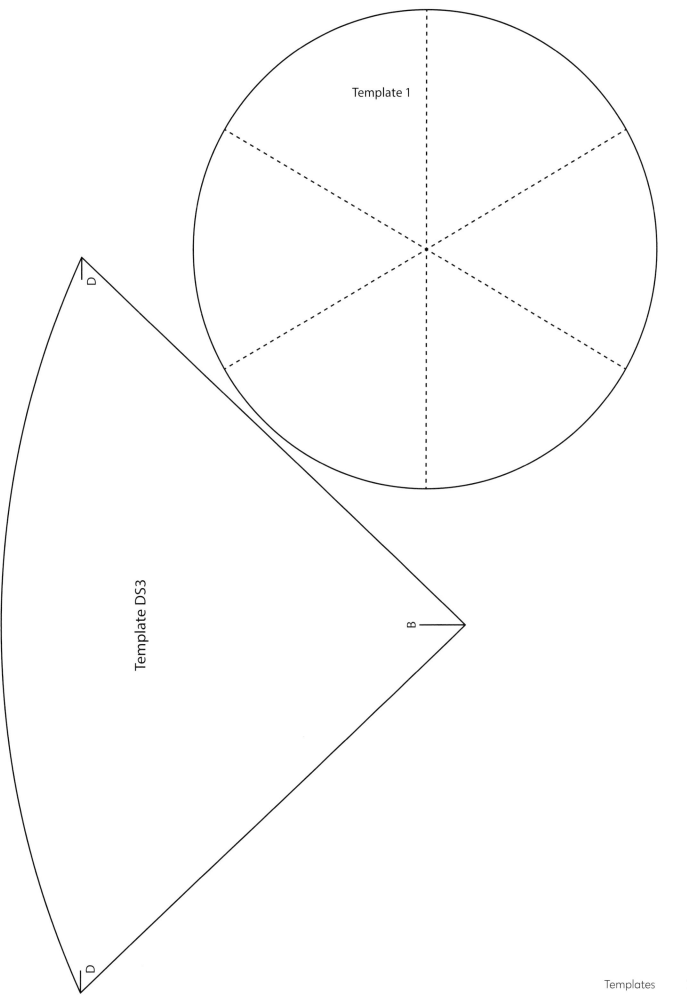

Template 1

Template DS3

D

D

B

about the AUTHOR

Crafting has been part of Kirsten's life since she was five years old. Her first project was a pillowcase made out of a Danish cleaning cloth with very loose loops that you could pull a string of yarn through. Then Kirsten's grandmother taught her how to knit at the age of seven. Sewing and knitting have been a part of Kirsten's life ever since.

In Denmark, where she was born, sewing was taught in school, and by the age of fourteen, Kirsten sewed a lot of her own clothes. When she moved to Brooklyn in 1977, her first sewing project was her wedding dress. It was made from hand-painted floral curtains from her grandmother's apartment in Copenhagen. After that, her mother-in-law bought her a sewing machine.

In 1983, Kirsten came upon the Brooklyn Quilters Guild show and fell in love with quilting. Creating beautiful usable objects really appealed to her. At the same time, quilting allowed her to explore the possibilities of geometric designs.

Kirsten has been teaching quilting and her original technique for fabric bowl making for more than ten years. Her pieces have been shown in galleries and museums in New York and New Jersey. She is a member and former copresident of the Brooklyn Quilters Guild and is a member of the Textile Study Group of New York. Kirsten is also the author of *Modern Fabric Art Bowls*.

Visit Kirsten online (kirstenfisher.net), and follow her on social media @7willowstudio.